OLD LONDON

Dixon's shop, photographed by his son, Thomas James.

OLD LONDON

PHOTOGRAPHED BY HENRY DIXON AND
ALFRED & JOHN BOOL FOR THE SOCIETY FOR
PHOTOGRAPHING RELICS OF OLD LONDON

GRAHAM BUSH

ACADEMY EDITIONS · LONDON
ST MARTIN'S PRESS · NEW YORK

I am grateful to John Fraser for his careful research into the life and work of Henry Dixon, and to the Guildhall Library for providing all the photographs except for 24a and 41a which were provided by the London Museum.

First published in Great Britain in 1975 by
Academy Editions 7 Holland Street London W8

SBN 85670 150 5

First published in the U.S.A. by St Martin's Press inc.
175 Fifth Avenue New York N.Y. 10010

Library of Congress Catalog Card Number 73-93021

Printed and bound in Great Britain by
Balding & Mansell Ltd, Wisbech and London

CONTENTS

HENRY DIXON

AND
THE SOCIETY FOR PHOTOGRAPHING RELICS
OF
OLD LONDON

The Society for Photographing Relics of Old London originated in the wish of a few friends to have a record of the Oxford Arms in Warwick Lane, threatened in 1873 and demolished in 1878. Negatives were made by Alfred and John Bool of Pimlico at the direction of Alfred Marks. Prints were made from six of these by Henry Dixon and Son of Albany Street and these were distributed among subscribers in 1875. Letters leading to the formation of the Society appeared in *The Times* of 1875:

Saturday 20 March page 11: a letter was printed from George H. Birch, President of the Architectural Association, pleading for the retention of the tower and spire of St. Antholin, Budge-row (which the local Vestry intended to demolish).

On Friday 5 March page 10 a letter entitled 'Roman London' appeared:

Sir, – The old London wall to which Mr. Loftus refers may be seen at the rear of Newgate, at the Oxford Arms Inn, Warwick-lane, Newgate-street, a quaint and ancient hostel, perhaps the oldest now extant. It is up a passage between 14 and 15, Warwick-lane.
    I am, Sir, yours, &c,   J.B.

On Saturday 6 March page 10:

Mr. Alfred Marks writes to us from Long Ditton:–'Will you allow me to say with reference to "J.B.'s" letter in *The Times* of Thursday, that the very picturesque old inn (of the 16th century, as I am told by architects), the Oxford Arms, Warwick-lane, is advertised for sale by auction. As its destruction at no distant date is, therefore, certain, a few gentlemen have combined in order to have a set of photographic views of it taken, and should any readers of *The Times* interested in London antiquities desire to join the subscription, I shall be happy to hear from them.'

And on Wednesday 7 April page 7:

'A.M.' writes to us:–'Within a few days a most interesting relic of old London will have disappeared. The materials of the houses Nos. 42 and 43, Lime-street, will be sold on Wednesday, those of Nos. 44 to 47 on the following day. The whole originally formed a large mansion, the date of which (1631) still appears on the gateway. Throughout all the houses, but especially in No. 47, are to be found specimens, probably as good as any in existence, of the architecture of the time. Panelling, ceilings, and chimney-pieces are all alike excellent and highly characteristic of the period, the last-mentioned a good judge supposes to be from the hand which executed those at Knowle. It is not too late for some of your London readers to visit the spot, but it is to be regretted that the Fishmongers' and Carpenters' Companies, to whom the property belongs, have not afforded the public greater opportunities of seeing for the last time one of the few really old houses of which London can still boast.'

There were further letters later in the year; one, from David Masson of Edinburgh, pleaded for the preservation of Milton's house at 19 York-street, Westminster (22 October), and one from E. Robson again attacked the decision to demolish the tower and spire of St. Antholin, Watling-street (8 November), which was supported by a letter from Charles Eastlake (9 November). In addition there was a considerable correspondence concerning the proposed widening of Rennie's London Bridge, which started with a letter of protest from G. E. Street on 18 September.

Reference to the proposed Society also appeared in two issues of the *Builder* in 1875. The issue of 27 February contained a report of the ordinary general meeting of the Architectural Association of London held on 19 February. The third paragraph reads as follows:

The President stated that he had received a communication from Mr. A. Marks to the effect that the Oxford Arms, Paternoster-row, was advertised for sale by auction, intimating that photographs of the building, one of the few old hostelries in London now remaining, would be on sale: four views would be taken, and the cost would not exceed 10*s*. 6*d*. per set.

The issue of 6 March contained the following letter:

The 'Oxford Arms'

Sir, – Will you allow me to say, with reference to your summary of a letter of mine which the president was good enough to read at the last meeting of the Architectural Association, that the photographs of the 'Oxford Arms' will not, strictly speaking, be on sale. At the request of a few gentlemen who combined in order to have views of this interesting old building taken, I, as one of the subscribers, undertook the arrangement of the matter, and shall be happy to receive the names of any gentlemen who would like to join the subscription.

Long Ditton   Alfred Marks

The first prints were well received and gained notice in *The Times*. The reviewer thought well of the prints, which in his opinion conveyed the drama and atmosphere of the ancient inn: photography was a fit medium in which all that was best of the past might be preserved.

The following extracts are from a report which appeared in *The Times* of Thursday 21 December 1876 on page 4:

Old London

On Monday evening, Mr. G. H. Birch, A.R.I.B.A., read by request, before the Royal Institute of British Architects – Mr. Henry Currey, V.P., in the chair – a paper, profusely illustrated, on the Domestic Architecture of London in the Seventeenth Century.

The report mentioned that Mr. Birch was dealing with two very different periods and styles of architecture, viz. those before and after the Great Fire; that Mr. Birch said the wards of Bishopsgate, Portsoken, Aldgate, Tower, Lime-street, and Broad-street were those which largely escaped the effects of the Great Fire and therefore contained many examples of the earlier period; and that Mr Birch mentioned specifically existing houses in Bishopsgate, especially Sir Paul Pindar's house, Half Moon-street, Great St. Helen's, Crosby Square, 25, Bishopsgate-street, Crosby-hall-chambers, and a house in Lime-street destroyed in 1872 but which he was able to record in drawings.

Some of the oldest London inns were passed in review, the Tabard, the Swan with Four Necks, or 'Nicks' rather, as Mr. Birch said it should be, and the Oxford Arms in Warwick-lane. The views of the last taken by the society for photographing Old London were exhibited, and their beauty of chiaroscuro was lovingly dwelt upon. The Oxford Arms was rebuilt immediately after the Great Fire, as a contemporary advertisement of Edward Bartlett, an Oxford carrier, whose headquarters the inn was, demonstrably proved. These old inns were built on a sort of traditional plan, so that the present Oxford Arms resembled the old model. Old river-side houses, ancient tenements in Hoxton High-street, Wapping, Blackwall, Aldgate, Mile End-road, and Gray's Inn-lane were next spoken of, and then followed more detailed accounts of Lambeth Palace, Middle Temple Hall, Lincoln's-Inn, Gray's-Inn, with a slight mention of the minor Inns of Court. The history and architecture of the Charterhouse were sketched more fully. Before concluding the lecturer spoke of 'one little gem of a room' in the Ward Schools of St. Botolph, Billingsgate, all panelled in oak, and in each of the panels an excellent painting in chiaroscuro in a very perfect state of preservation. Attention was also called to a house in Mark-lane – not the well known old house on the right going from Fenchurch-street, but on the left, close to the Corn Exchange, in which there was a very perfect room, with a high chimney-piece, elaborate architrave and pediments to the door, with a very richly-decorated plaster ceiling. Unhappily, it was about to be pulled down. The paper was repeatedly cheered, and a discussion followed.

The Society was encouraged to continue its work and yearly issues followed, taking as their subjects buildings the Society believed were threatened with demolition. During the twelve years of its existence the Society issued 120 photographs and made many representations to various companies to prevent the destruction of buildings it considered worth preserving. Many of these still remain; others were demolished around the turn of the century and more were demolished before negatives could be made.

There is some confusion as to the exact date of the demolition in some cases, especially in that of the Oxford Arms. Several books on inns give the date as 1875. The usually authoritative Wheatley (*London Past and Present*, 1891 edition) says that it was sold in 1875 and pulled down in 1876. Yet Alfred Marks, in his notes to the photographs of the Society says it was demolished in 1877. The notes are dated 1881 which is nearer to the date of demolition than the records of the other writers.

The evidence of the contemporary rate books for the Ward of Farringdon Without are of interest here. Unfortunately there was a consolidated rate for the whole year so a more precise time cannot be arrived at than that of a whole year. The rate book for the year 1877, under the Oxford Arms Passage, lists at No. 4 Louisa Briden as the occupier 'including the Inn'. The rate book for the following year, 1878, at the same number has the one word 'Down' written against it, which indicates that the Inn had been demolished by the end of 1877.

Life is never simple and certainly not for the researcher. The evidence of the rate books appears to be contradicted and yet confirmed by the Land Tax assessment books for the same period. These list a 'Hotel & Yard' for each year from 1876 to 1879 under the title of Oxford Arms Passage, but confirmation of a sort can be deduced from the disappearance of the name of an occupier. For the year 1876 the occupier is given as 'Briden'; for the year 1877 the occupier is given as 'Late Briden'. In the books for the years 1878 and 1879 no name is given at all.

The evidence of the rate books can be supported by the entries in the City of London Directory published by W. H. & L. Collingridge each year. In the issue for 1877 in the details given for Oxford Arms Passage the west side of the Passage is said to be '*Oxford Arms*, William Briden'. Nine other names are listed as the occupants of the Oxford Arms Passage. In the issue for 1878 there is no entry for the Oxford Arms Inn and there are only three names given for occupants in the Passage, and even in the issue for 1879 two names still appear for people residing in the Passage.

Further confirmation for a date of 1877 for the demolition of the Inn can be found in Augustus Hare's *Walks In London*. This book was published in 1878 but consisted mainly of articles that he had already published, as he pointed out in his preface – which was dated November 1877 which brings us even closer to the date of demolition. Hare's description of the Oxford Arms Inn begins thus:

'Opposite the Bell, closing an alley on the left, stood the Oxford Arms, one of the most curious old hostelries in England, demolished in 1877.'

In 1879 the annual issue was enlarged to include twelve prints, this time taken and printed by Henry Dixon, as were all those in subsequent issues. A descriptive letterpress was distributed in 1881 to accompany the existing prints, and this was added to as new prints appeared until the Society ceased its activities in 1886.

Surviving buildings are mostly connected with the church or the law. Almost all of the inns and street views have disappeared with the way of life that called them into being. Half-timber houses were altered over the years to become candle factories, ironmongeries, or anything else their owners wished to make of them, and finally fell into shambles and were demolished, to be replaced by banks or offices. Travellers had no need for coaching inns and stayed at the railway hotel with its substantial brick and tile. Carriers, too, lost their trade to the railways and no longer needed the inns that had served them for centuries. The inns were rented out, not repaired and in the end demolished. Tenants of the Oxford Arms can be seen peering into the camera, their dwellings already precarious, looking as if they were camping out in the shrine of some long vanished deity.

The photographs often contain activity. Figures stare at the camera, moving perhaps an arm to leave a smear on the plate. Some have obviously been told to stand still; others go about their business unconscious of the camera. Sometimes carts stay long enough to register on the plate, and sometimes they pass leaving tracks in the air. Fast emulsions would have lost these qualities, which for me are important. Photographers of that time, however, went to great lengths to keep their subjects still and exposures as short as possible, bearing in mind the demands that depth of field makes on exposure times. The time scale implied in the photograph gives its subject a past, present and future. This is clearly seen in the photographs of Dixon and the Bools, whereas modern photographers tend to snap at their subjects, leaving them in a sort of isolation. Dixon and the Bools never try to blind us with their art. The view presented is clear and without any sentimental overlay; they never impose themselves between the viewer and the subject, and so the photographs are in the best sense objective.

'Photographing in London is not easy', Henry Dixon wrote when introducing an account of how he obtained a negative in a crowded street. He used to remove a wheel from a covered wagon and while his assistants pretended to mend it he was able to photograph his subject from under the canvas.

Henry Dixon, one of the Society's main photographers, was born on 14 April 1820, the son of Thomas Dixon and Elizabeth Sutton. His parents had married at Old St. Pancras Church in 1800 and Henry who was the youngest of ten children was baptised there on 29 July 1821. His father, according to indentures dated 29 September 1790 and 18 March 1796, was a master copperplate printer, and by the time the second child, Thomas, was born (29 November 1802) he was foreman at Alderman Boydell's Cheapside printing establishment, so a note in a book of engravings printed by Thomas Junior records. The father died on 9 March 1832; perhaps family memories became a little dim over the years, or perhaps he had changed his occupation towards the end of his life, but in the marriage certificate of Henry Dixon he is described as a carpenter.

Henry's elder brother, Thomas, became a copperplate printer and at one time worked at Messrs Colnaghi & Sons, 23 Cockspur Street, again according to a note in the book of engravings. In 1833 he went into partnership with his friend Thomas Ross as copperplate printers in a workshop at the back of a house in Hampstead Road. They worked for artists and engravers and made maps. Their business appears in Kelly's Post Office Street Directory for 1838 as being at 4 St. James's Place, Hampstead Road, Somers Town; according to Kelly's the business was at No. 4 until 1863, and also at No. 7 from 1858; then from 1864 their business was in the Hampstead Road, first at No. 70, then in the following year also at No. 76. Thomas Dixon died in 1875 and Henry was one of the executors of his will.

Henry started by being apprenticed to his brother Thomas. He bound himself apprentice to Thomas Dixon and Thomas Ross 'to learn their Art...from the First day of January 1836 until the full End & Term of Seven years', according to his indenture. He was to receive wages of five shillings a week from 1 January 1836 to 1 January 1837, one quarter of the price received by his brother and his partner for his services from 1 January 1837 to 1 January 1840 and then one half of the same from 1 January 1840 to 1 January 1843. According to the census of 1841 he lived with his brother's family. In 1846 Thomas and Henry Dixon and some friends started a property investment company on 1 December and, according to the company's report, their address was 3 St. James's Place, Hampstead Road. Later reports of this company are useful in tracing Henry Dixon's various addresses.

When Henry first met his wife we do not know, but a poem that he wrote to her entitled *Hope* still survives and is dated 18 November 1846. However we do know that Henry married Sophia Cook on 18 September 1848. Her father, James Cook, was roasting cook to the Duke of York and then an innkeeper and butcher at Byfleet, Surrey. Their marriage certificate states Henry's occupation as being that of copperplate printer. The marriage was a fruitful one as they had nine children. His wife survived him; she was left everything in his will and died on 28 April 1916.

Henry's eldest son, Thomas James, was born on 24 September 1857; he was eventually to join his father in his photographic work, and to carry it on after Henry's death.

Exactly when Henry Dixon became a photographer is difficult to determine. On his son's birth certificate in 1857 Henry is described as 'Copper Plate Printer (Journeyman)'. His name first occurs in Kelly's for 1864 when he was established at 56 Albany Street, Regent's Park, NW as a Photographer. Previously he had been living at Watford, with 7 St. James's Place as his business address, as the company reports show; and the report for 2 November 1864 confirms the address given in Kelly's. This was the address he was to remain at for the rest of his professional life. The numbering of the street was changed so that from 1866 he was at No. 112, but the building was the one he occupied from 1864. The rate books show that his brother Thomas at first paid the rates for him. From a photograph which Henry took in later years we know that he had a shop at 112 Albany Street; presumably he lived above this shop with his wife and ever increasing number of children, as they all appear at this address in the census of 1871. At that date the two eldest daughters, then aged 20 and 19, seem to have helped him in his work as ditto marks appear against their names under the word 'Photographer' which is written against Henry's name. Thomas James, then aged 13, is described as a 'Scholar'.

Tradition within the Dixon family records that Henry Dixon, apart from his series of photographs of old London, photographed private art collections and that also he was one of the inventors of panchromatic photography in the sense of representing colours by different shades in black-and-white photography. In common with many Victorian middle class families, the Dixon family liked parties, dressing-up and musical evenings.

Thomas James became his father's partner in 1886 as the entry in Kelly's for that year is changed from 'Henry Dixon' to 'Henry Dixon & Son'. When Henry retired cannot be said for sure. That he did retire we know from his death certificate on which he is described as 'Photographer Master retired'. He died on 20 January 1893 at 117 Chetwynd Road, Kentish Town, and as his will was dated a year earlier, 9 February 1892, from this address it is perhaps safe to conclude that by that date he was living there in retirement. The rate books show that his son replaced him as the rate payer for 112 Albany Street in 1892. The cause of death is given very clearly and in a precise, logical order on the certificate: 'Stammering Heart years Influenza 18 months Bronchial Catarrh 1 week Paralysis of Heart 1 minute'. It seems likely that the onset of the influenza was the factor that brought about Henry Dixon's retirement.

How highly did Henry Dixon prize his work as a photographer? We cannot, of course, be sure. But we know from what he says about photography that he felt there were clear dividing lines between photography and engraving with certain areas appropriate to each art. And in his will, made almost a year before his death, he described himself as 'copper-plate printer', so perhaps he basically felt that his original calling was the more important one.

How strongly he may have felt about this we do not know, but we do know that Henry Dixon made more out of his photography than his brother Thomas did out of printing. Thomas Dixon's effects in 1875 were under £800. Henry Dixon's effects were £1,098 1s. 7d.

The firm of Henry Dixon & Son was carried on by Thomas James until the Second World War. The entries in Kelly's appear for 112 Albany Street until 1941 but the rate books show that the firm was only there until 1939 – possibly for the last two years the firm was renting No. 112 as in 1941 the firm moved to Rose & Crown Yard in SW1. But even here there is a conflict between the evidence of the rate books and of Kelly's.

The entries in Kelly's are for Nos. 3 and 4 from 1941 to 1944, the rate books show that Henry Dixon & Son Ltd. were at No. 10 in a ground floor stable for the quarters ending September 1941 and March 1942.

Thomas James Dixon must have retired at the latest early in 1942 as his will, which was dated 3 February 1942, describes him as 'photographer retired'. By this time he was living at Chetwynd, 27 King Edwards Road, Ware, in Hertfordshire. He died on 25 February 1943, leaving no children and distributing his estate among his nephews and nieces, the widow of his brother and one cousin. Among the named legacies were the photographs of London, their quality and intrinsic interest being recognised by Henry's son at the end of his career.

Henry Dixon was commissioned to do a special series of Old London photographs by Franz James Mankiewicz, who mentions them in his will. Mankiewicz, of 2 Whitehall Court, SW, died on 24 February 1917 at a nursing home at 15 Henrietta-street, Cavendish-square. His sister, Alice Sedgwick, married in 1888 Sir Julius Charles Wernher, the first Baronet; hence he was an uncle of the late Sir Harold Augustus Wernher, G.C.V.O., T.D., the third Baronet.

'To my friend Albert Forbes Sieveking £400 and all the negatives of the photographs of London taken for me by Henry Dixon and Son of 112 Albany Street NW now in their possession and which belong to me and also the duplicates of the said photographs on cards which are in my possession in my Flat.' . . .

From Clause 8: . . . 'the collection of framed London Topographical Prints each one marked in the right-hand bottom corner with my private stamp (and no other which have not got this stamp on)' were left to the London Museum but with general conditions, such as that they should all be in frames and hung at the same time with a notice saying that the collection was formed and presented by Mr. Mankiewicz, and should these conditions not be accepted the collection was to be offered to the L.C.C., the Guildhall Museum, the City of Westminster, the Tate Gallery, the British Museum and the Victoria & Albert Museum, in that order.

From Clause 9: . . . 'the collection of photographs of London taken specially for me by the said Henry Dixon and Son and which are in an Album bearing the title *Old London Photographed for F. J. Mankiewicz 1910* and also my Album bearing the title *Society for the photographing of Relics of Old London*' were left to the London Museum – and may be seen there now if one makes an application beforehand in writing.

The most important legacy of the Society is the prints themselves. All of these are reproduced here in the order in which they first appeared with section headings for each of the twelve issues. Where buildings have been demolished, the date of demolition is given. Parts of the original text are included where they are not overlong or too concerned with the attribution of the buildings to Inigo Jones.

The letter (*a*) beside the number of a print indicates that the photograph was not included in the original series but formed part of the special series photographed for Franz James Mankiewicz. No. 24(*a*) and the frontispiece, of Dixon's Shop, were photographed by Thomas James Dixon at a later date.

Graham Bush

SECTION 1
PHOTOGRAPHS OF
THE OXFORD
ARMS IN
WARWICK LANE

BY ALFRED AND JOHN BOOL
PRINTED IN PERMANENT
PIGMENTS BY HENRY DIXON
FIRST ISSUED IN 1875

NOTES TO PLATES 1-6

1. The entrance of the Oxford Arms from Warwick Lane
Demolished 1878

The inn stood in a short lane leading out of the west side of Warwick Lane until its demolition.

Up to the time of its close it still did a considerable carriers' business, carts daily leaving the Inn for Oxford and other places. An old servant of the Inn told the writer that, in the days before the railroads, he had frequently seen wagons drawn by nine horses leave the Inn, a portion of the goods being packed after the Inn yard had been cleared. It must have needed careful handling to get such a team and such a load safely round the corner of the narrow street.

2. The inn yard
Demolished 1903

A writer in the Athenaeum *of May 20, 1876 said: 'Despite the confusion, the dirt, and the decay, he who stands in the yard of this ancient Inn may get an excellent idea of what it was like in the days of its prosperity, when not only travellers in coach and saddle rode into and out of the yard, but poor players and mountebanks set up their stage for the entertainment of spectators, who hung over the galleries or looked on from their "rooms" – a name by which the boxes of a theatre were first known.'*

3. The entrance looking towards Warwick Lane
Demolished 1878

As to the name Warwick Lane two passages in Stow's Survey *give pictures so curious to read in this nineteenth century that it is impossible to resist the temptation to quote them. 'This is Eldenesse Lane which stretcheth north to the high street of Newgate Market; the same is now called Warwicke Lane, of an ancient house there built by the Earl of Warwicke . . . It is in record called a messuage in Eldenesse Lane, in the parish of St. Sepulchre, the 28th of Henry VI.' Warwick Square now stands on the site of this house.*

4. A view along the upper gallery
Demolished 1878

The sumptuous furniture of the Inn was sold in 1868, since which time its many rooms were let out in tenements. The site is now occupied by the new building and gardens of the Minor Canons of St. Paul's.

5. A staircase on an enlarged scale
Demolished 1878

Richard Nevill, Earl of Warwick, came 'with six hundred men, all in red jackets, embroidered with ragged staves before and behind, and was lodged in Warwicke lane; in whose house there was oftentimes six oxen eaten at breakfast, and every tavern was full of his meat; for he that had any acquaintance in that house might have there so much of sodden and roasted meat as he prick and carry upon a long dagger.'

6. A general view of the inn from the windows of the Old Bailey looking towards St. Paul's
Demolished 1878

The London Gazette of 1672 tells of an Oxford carrier who moved to the Oxford Arms after the destruction of his inn during the Great Fire: 'These are to give notice that Edward Bartlet, Oxford Carrier, hath removed his Inn in London from the Swan at Holborn Bridge to the Oxford Arms in Warwick Lane, where he did Inn before the Fire. His coaches and wagons going forth on their usual days, Mondays, Wednesdays, and Fridays. He hath also a hearse with all things convenient to carry a Corps to any part of England.'

6a. A view of the inn yard taken in 1876 by Henry Dixon
Demolished 1903

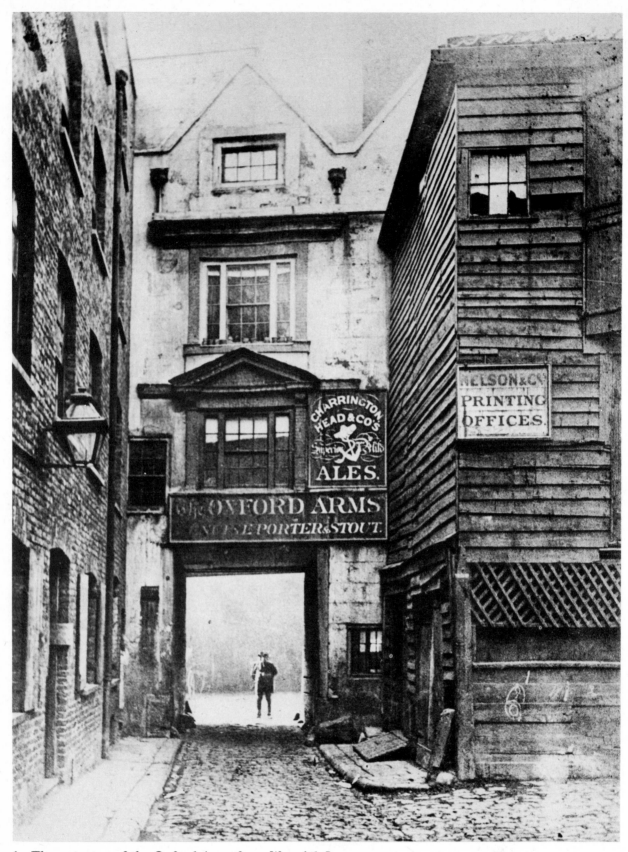

1. The entrance of the Oxford Arms from Warwick Lane

Demolished 1878

2. The inn yard

Demolished 1903

3. The entrance looking towards Warwick Lane

Demolished 1878

4. **A view along the upper gallery**

Demolished 1878

5. A staircase on an enlarged scale

Demolished 1878

6. A general view of the inn from the windows of the Old Bailey looking towards St. Paul's
Demolished 1878

6a. A view of the inn yard taken in 1876 by Henry Dixon

Demolished 1903

SECTION 2
PHOTOGRAPHS OF OLD HOUSES IN WYCH STREET AND LINCOLN'S INN

BY ALFRED AND JOHN BOOL
PRINTED IN PERMANENT
PIGMENTS BY HENRY DIXON
FIRST ISSUED IN 1876

NOTES TO PLATES 7–12

7. Old houses in Wych Street looking east towards St. Clement Danes

Demolished 1903

The name of this street, a continuation of Drury Lane, is seemingly derived from the termination of the street Aldewich. Via de Aldewych, now Drury Lane, gave its name to the land adjoining it on both sides, and was of very great antiquity. These are very good specimens of the overhanging houses of the beginning of the seventeenth century.

8. Old houses in Wych street looking west

Demolished 1903

9. Old houses in Drury Lane

Demolished 1890

That with the gables was formerly a public house, the Cock and Magpie (so figured in Archer's Vestiges of Old London) *originally the Cock and Pye. A writer in the* European Magazine *for 1807, vol.52, where also an illustration is given, says that the tradition, derived from very old persons, who had long been dead, asserts that this was known as a place of entertainment in the reign of Henry VII. It then looked over the fields. Towards the close of the reign of James I, the house at the upper end of Wych Street began to be built. Probably no part of the existing house is of earlier date than the first half of the seventeenth century. The Cock and Pye in Drury Lane seems to have been distinct from the public-house with the same sign which gave its name to the Cock and Pye Fields, the site of the Seven Dials (Parton's* History of St. Giles in the Fields).

10. Drury Lane looking towards St. Mary-le-Strand

(The previous view reversed). Demolished 1890

The narrow turning leading to the church from Drury Lane, now Drury Court, was at one time known as Maypole Lane. There were great rejoicings when, in 1661, after puritannical rigours, a Maypole 134 ft. high was here erected, 'by the gracious consent of his majesty Charles II.' 'as near hand as they guess in the very same pit where the former stood, but far more glorious, bigger and higher than ever any that stood before it.' 'Ancient people did clap their hands saying. "Golden days begin to appear".'

11. Lincoln's Inn Gate House

Rebuilt to the original design after the Second World War

Lincoln's Inn takes its name from Henry Lacy, Earl of Lincoln, who in the thirteenth century built here his 'inn' or 'house' as we should now say, on the site of Black Friars. 'This Lincoln's Inn' says Stow, '... is now an Inn of Court, retaining the name of Lincoln's Inn as afore, but now lately increased with fair buildings ... In the reign of Henry VIII, Sir Thomas Lovell was a great builder there; especially he built the gatehouse of one front towards the East, placing thereon as well the Lacie's arms as his own.' The Gate House shown in the Photograph is that spoken of by Stow. The date 1518 can be read below the arms.

12. Lincoln's Inn Old Square

Largely demolished. A few fragments remain

Old buildings erected at various times between the reigns of Henry VII and James I. The buttresses to the left of the photograph form part of Inigo Jones' chapel, an example of what came to be known as 'bastard Gothic'.

7. Old houses in Wych Street looking east towards St. Clement Danes

Demolished 1903

8. Old houses in Wych street looking west
Demolished 1903

9. Old houses in Drury Lane

Demolished 1890

10. Drury Lane looking towards St. Mary-le-Strand
(The previous view reversed). Demolished 1890

11. Lincoln's Inn Gate House

Rebuilt to the original design after the Second World War

12. Lincoln's Inn Old Square

Largely demolished. A few fragments remain

SECTION 3
PHOTOGRAPHS OF
ST BARTHOLOMEWS
AND CLOTH FAIR

BY ALFRED AND JOHN BOOL
PRINTED IN PERMANENT
PIGMENTS BY HENRY DIXON
FIRST ISSUED IN 1877

13. St. Bartholomew's churchyard and tower

The object of the present series is not to give a record of the church itself. The noble work of the interior, its massive Norman arches, grand proportions and magnificent tombs, could be far better rendered by the art of the etcher. Our aim — and we may in future numbers return to the subject; by no means exhausted in this set — has rather been to show the picturesque manner in which the ecclesiastical and civil buildings are, as it were, dovetailed together in the quaintest nook of Old London.

14. The churchyard looking towards Cloth Fair

Cloth Fair, though it has undergone alterations in recent years still preserves, far beyond any other portion of London, mediaeval characteristics. Here are narrow walled lanes, where two persons can pass one another with difficulty. In another the occupants of one house could literally, and without danger or difficulty, shake hands from windows on opposite sides of the way. The explorer may thread covered passages from which he can note details of domestic life passing within easy ken. That houses built so closely, and of such inflammable material, should have survived to the present day seems little short of marvellous.

15. The Green churchyard on the site of the old south transept

Demolished 1891

Vast as the existing church is, it is little more than one-third of the Priory founded in the twelfth century. At the dissolution of monasteries, so much of the Priory Church as had not been demolished was assigned to the inhabitants of the great close of St. Bartholomew.

16. A window at the east end of the church and the boys' school built over the north aisle of the choir

Demolished early 1900s

17. The north side of the church and the Poors' Churchyard

(Taken with the light behind it.) Demolished early 1900s

18. The Poors' Churchyard

Demolished early 1900s

The camera now looks into the light toward some figures, one in the gateway from which the previous view was taken and one on the wall beside.

13. St. Bartholomew's churchyard and tower

14. The churchyard looking towards Cloth Fair

15. The Green churchyard on the site of the old south transept

Demolished 1891

16. A window at the east end of the church and the boys' school built over the north aisle of the choir
Demolished early 1900's

17. The north side of the church and the Poors' Churchyard

(Taken with the light behind it.) Demolished early 1900's

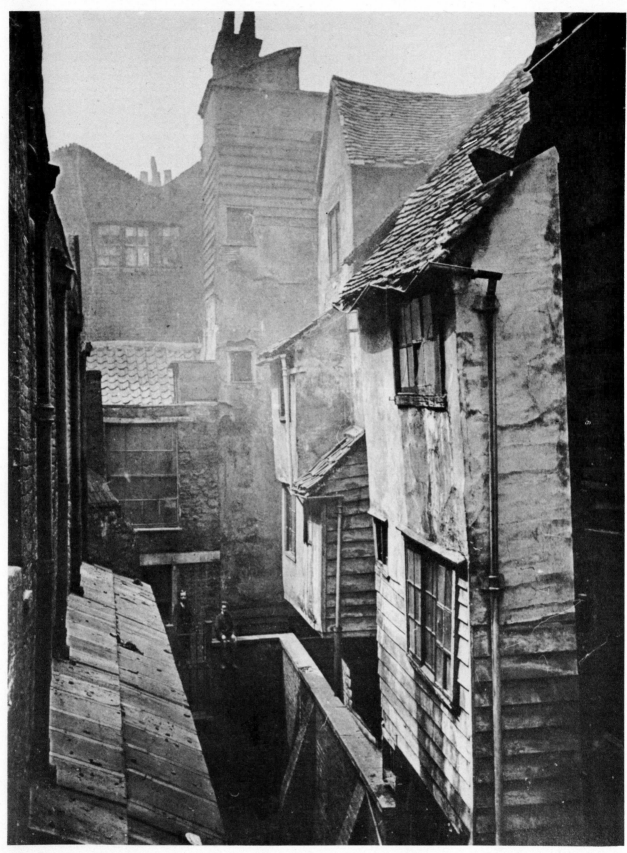

18. The Poors' Churchyard
Demolished early 1900's

SECTION 4 PHOTOGRAPHS OF TEMPLE BAR, HOUSES IN GRAY'S INN LANE AND HOLBORN, A SHOP IN BREWER STREET AND THE SIR PAUL PINDAR IN BISHOPSGATE STREET

BY ALFRED AND JOHN BOOL
PRINTED IN PERMANENT
PIGMENTS BY HENRY DIXON
FIRST ISSUED IN 1878

NOTES TO PLATES 19–24

19. The Temple Bar
Dismantled in 1878 and removed to Hertfordshire

The Bar as we saw it till it was replaced by the 'Memorial' and its famous 'Griffin', was built from Wren's designs in 1670. Over the gateway on the East side were statues of Elizabeth and James I; the statues on the West side, shown in our photograph, were of Charles I and Charles II 'in Roman habits'. All the Gates of London, except Newgate and Temple Bar, being taken down in the years 1760–1761, heads of 'traitors' which it had been the practice to exhibit at London Bridge – Hentzner, travelling in England in 1597 counted over thirty on the Southwark Gate – were afterwards stuck on Temple Bar.

20. Leadenhall Street
Demolished 1876

The iron gate and courtyard of a very fine mansion, demolished in 1875 or 1876. The house and its contiguous warehouse and courtyards, occupying a great area, were for many years occupied by a firm of wholesale druggists, Messrs. Baiss Brothers, who always most courteously allowed strangers to see the house. It was no doubt in its day – the beginning of the eighteenth century the residence of a great merchant . . . The fittings and decorations of this house were of a very sumptuous character. A great room on the first floor was panelled in cedar; the grand staircase was particularly fine, the landing being of parquetry, and the walls handsomely decorated by Thornhill or his assistants. These wall paintings are now in South Kensington Museum.

21. Old houses in Gray's Inn Lane
Demolished 1878

Opposite to the entrance of the Verulam Buildings in Gray's Inn. The houses were demolished very soon after the taking of this photograph for the purpose of widening the street. One of the group of houses bore on a carved corbel a date towards the close of the sixteenth century. These houses must have been on the verge of London in this part for more than a century; maps of the beginning of the eighteenth century showing very little extension of building north of Liquorpond Street.

22. Shop in Brewer Street
This photograph shows an old-fashioned shop, date early eighteenth century, of a style very few examples of which are now left. Brewer Street was built about 1680, Soho being then, as it long remained, a fashionable part of the town.

23. The Sir Paul Pindar, Bishopsgate Street
Since the photograph was taken, the house on the spectator's left, marked as the site of a new hospital, has been destroyed. It contained a superb ceiling, which on representations made by this Society, was secured by the South Kensington Museum. The style of this ceiling, exactly corresponding with the one in the public house next door, seems to leave no doubt – though the question has been raised – that this house also formed part of the magnificent mansion erected in the reign of James I by Sir Paul Pindar, one of the greatest and wealthiest merchant princes of his day. One of his achievements was the introduction into this country of the method of making allum, or 'allom' as it was then spelt, which had before his time been imported from abroad.

24. Staple Inn, Holborn Front
'Behind the most ancient part of Holborn' says Dickens, 'where certain gabled houses, some centuries of age, still stand looking on the public way, as if disconsolately looking for the Old Bourne that has long run dry.' This is in truth one of the most picturesque groups of Old London houses. They are also among the oldest, dating apparently from the time of James I, or perhaps somewhat earlier, for Stow writing in 1598 of the Staple Inn says.' 'The same of late is for a great part thereof fair built and not a little augmented.' The obelisk, topped by a lamp, marks the City boundary. Just here opposite Gray's Inn lane, stood, till a few years back, Middle Row, narrowing the thoroughfare and blocking the traffic. This was the most famous and obvious example in London – a few are still left, Holywell Street being perhaps one – of 'Middle Rows', encroachments on the highway where this was originally sufficiently broad to allow the erection of temporary structures, which in time gave way to permanent buildings.

24a. Staple Inn, restored, as it appeared in 1911
The Victorians thought timber and frame buildings ought to be painted black and white. Many buildings now treated in this way were originally allowed to weather, the wood receiving little treatment and the wattle being painted in pastel shades covering most of the timber.

19. The Temple Bar

Dismantled and removed to Hertfordshire

20. Leadenhall Street

Demolished 1876

21. Old houses in Gray's Inn Lane

Demolished 1878

22. **Shop in Brewer Street**

23. The Sir Paul Pindar, Bishopsgate Street

24. Staple Inn, Holborn Front

Old House "Staples Inn" Holborn, taken in 1910

24a. Staple Inn, restored, as it appeared in 1911

SECTION 5
PHOTOGRAPHS OF CANONBURY TOWER, BARNARD'S INN, OLD HOUSES IN ALDERSGATE STREET, CHRIST'S HOSPITAL AND THE CHURCHYARD OF ST LAWRENCE POUNTNEY

BY HENRY DIXON PRINTED IN
PERMANENT PIGMENTS FROM
HIS OWN NEGATIVES
FIRST ISSUED IN 1879

NOTES TO PLATES 25–36

25. Canonbury Tower
The Manor of Canonbury was an appendage of the Priory of St. Bartholomew, and appears to have been given to the Priory by Ralph de Berners, in the time of Edward I. The manorial house, rebuilt by the last Prior, or last but one, of St. Bartholomew, Prior Bolton with his 'bolt' and 'ton', was at the dissolution of religious houses given by Henry VIII to Thomas Cromwell. After several changes it came in 1570 into the possession of Sir John Spencer, who built the tower shown in our photographs.

26. Canonbury Tower
Here according to Sir John Hawkins, not a very trustworthy authority, Goldsmith wrote The Vicar of Wakefield: '*Of the booksellars whom he styled his friends, Mr. Newbury was one. This person had apartments in Canonbury House, where Goldsmith often lay concealed from his creditors. Under a pressing necessity he there wrote his* Vicar of Wakefield.'

27. Barnard's Inn Hall
The Hall is said to have been built not later than 1450, but, as we now see it, it has undergone much alteration. It is remarkable as having preserved its louvre of lead of the time of Henry VIII, in its original condition. This is one of the few still remaining. Even after the halls were furnished with fireplaces in the side walls, the practice was continued of kindling a fire on a hearth of tile or brick in the centre of the room, letting the smoke escape through a hole in the roof, over which was an erection to keep out the rain, with open sides - the louvre.

28. Barnard's Inn, the courtyard
To those who know the quiet retirement and old-world air of Barnard's Inn, it will seem in accordance with the fitness of things that the last of the alchemists should have pursued here his search for the elixir. This was Peter Woulfe, a Fellow of the Royal Society, who died in 1805. 'Sir Humphrey Davy tells us', says Mr. Timbs in his Century of Anecdotes '*that he used to hang up written prayers and inscriptions of recommendations of his processes to Providence. His chambers were so filled with furnaces and apparatus, that it was difficult to reach the fireside.' He breakfasted at four in the morning; friends were admitted only upon giving a secret signal.*

29. Barnard's Inn, the Fetter Lane front
Demolished 1910
Pip, of Great Expectations, *at one time had his quarters in what Dickens rather harshly calls 'the dingiest collection of shabby buildings ever squeezed together in a rank corner as a club for tom-cats.'*

30. Old houses in **Aldersgate Street**
Demolished 1879
The Legend, 'Shakespeare House' should not be taken seriously.

31. Old houses in **Aldersgate Street**
Demolished 1890
Examples of early seventeenth century architecture.

32. Shaftesbury House, Aldersgate Street
Demolished 1882
Thanet House . . . is now known as Shaftesbury House. It was built about 1644 by Inigo Jones. This house has had varied fortunes. From the Earls of Thanet is passed to Anthony Ashley Cooper, afterwards first Earl of Shaftesbury, Dryden's 'Achitophel' and one of the Cabal Ministry, whence its present name. At the beginning of the eighteenth century it came again into the possession of the Thanet family, was afterwards an inn and a tavern, and in 1750 became a Lying-in-Hospital, and subsequently a Dispensary.

33. Christ's Hospital
Demolished 1902
The entrance from Christ Church Passage, Newgate Street.

34. Christ's Hospital
Demolished 1902
The front overlooking the old burial ground of Christ Church, formerly the nave of the great church of Grey Friars Monastery.

35. Churchyard of St. Lawrence, Pountney
The Church in old times possessed the finest tower and spire within the limits of the City, and was a most conspicuous object in the beautiful view across the river from Bankside. It was destroyed in the Great Fire and not rebuilt, but portions of its wall are still to be seen in the fronts of the houses at the north-west corner of the Churchyard. This is the most picturesque perhaps, of all the City churchyards, so admirably described by Dickens in his Uncommercial

Traveller *Those to whom it is unknown would scarcely believe that it is but a stone's throw from Canon Street and the huge railway station, one of the busiest centres of London life. But the Churchyard was in its day a busy, even tumultuous place. Mr. Riley* (Memorials of London Life) *gives a petition to the Lord Mayor and Aldermen, presented by the poor Commonalty of the Weavers Flemings in 1370, the result of which was, that in order to prevent fights, which had been too common, it was decreed that the Weavers Flemings should hold their meetings for the hire of serving-men in this Churchyard, as they had been wont to do, while the weavers of Brabant were to hold their meetings for the like purpose in the Churchyard of St. Mary Somerset.*

36. Great Queen Street

Great Queen Street, built about 1629 from the designs either of Inigo Jones or his pupil, Webb, was so called from Henrietta Maria, Queen of Charles I. The street was then, and for some time afterwards, occupied by people of rank. Here was Conway House, the residence of the noble family of that name. Here lived the Marquis of Winchester, Lord Herbert of Cherbury, the Marquis of Worcester, and the Earl of Bristol, whose mansion taken in 1671 for the Board of Trade and Plantations, had seven rooms on a floor, a long gallery, gardens.

25. Canonbury Tower

26. Canonbury Tower

27. Barnard's Inn Hall

28. Barnard's Inn, the courtyard

29. Barnard's Inn, the Fetter Lane front

Demolished 1910

30. Old houses in Aldersgate Street

Demolished 1879

31. Old houses in Aldersgate Street

Demolished 1890

32. Shaftesbury House, Aldersgate Street

Demolished 1882

33. Christ's Hospital

Demolished 1902

34. Christ's Hospital

Demolished 1902

35. Churchyard of St. Lawrence, Pountney

36. Great Queen Street

SECTION 6
PHOTOGRAPHS OF THE CHARTERHOUSE, CHARTERHOUSE SQUARE, WASHHOUSE COURT AND THE CLOISTERS

BY HENRY DIXON PRINTED IN
PERMANENT PIGMENTS FROM
HIS OWN NEGATIVES
FIRST ISSUED IN 1880

37. General view from Charterhouse Square

On the spectator's left is the gateway, a Tudor arch with a dripstone terminating in corbels, and a shelf supported by two lions, the work of the early part of the sixteenth century. (Roper). *Archdeacon Hale in his explanation of a plan of the Monastery, of a date somewhat later than 1430, says: 'We find two kitchens mentioned ... the second, the building numbered 3, the remains of which are to be found in the wall next the present gateway of the Charterhouse, formed of squares of flint and stone.' In the description on the roll containing the plan, this kitchen is quaintly named 'Egipte, the fleyshe kychyne.'*

38. Washhouse Court

Thomas Sutton purchased the Charterhouse estates in 1611 for £13,000. He had for some years been bent on employing his fortune to the public good but until his purchase of Charterhouse his plan came to nothing. He used to pray: 'Lord, thou hast given me a large and liberal estate; give me also a heart to make use thereof.'

Sutton's scheme comprised a hospital for poor men and a free school for instructing, teaching, and maintenance of poor children and scholars. The first assembly of governors held in July 1613, decided, in accordance with Sutton's intentions, that no children should be admitted to the school 'whose parents had any estate in land to leave them, but only the children of poor men that wanted means to bring them up.'

39. Washhouse Court

The letters J. H. on the external wall are the initials of the last Prior but one, John Houghton, who suffered torture and execution during the Dissolution. All but one of his brethren died in prison; the survivor was later executed. Prior Trafford, who followed Houghton, brought about the surrender of the house obtaining a pension of twenty pounds a year. The buildings were then used to store the king's tents until the king, having another place for his tents, gave the estate to Lord North, then Sir Edward North. The Charterhouse passed through various hands until Thomas, Lord Howard sold it to Sutton.

40. The Cloisters

The atmosphere of the old monastery is preserved in the Cloisters although some alterations were made by the Duke of Norfolk who lived here from 1565 until his execution.

41. Second court with a view of the exterior wall of the Great Hall

41a Inner Gate from first to second court

This print was not issued with the other prints in this section but has been included to show how progress was made from the first to the second courtyard. The doorway of the Great Hall can be seen across the courtyard through the inner gate.

42. Interior

The hall was used at the time of the photograph as the pensioners' dining room. The Renaissance interior shows the influence of the Duke of Norfolk who regarded it as a home and endowed it with his personality.

43. Interior, looking towards the screen and musicians' gallery

44. Chimney-piece

The chimney-piece was added by Thomas Sutton whose office as master of ordinance is alluded to by the cannon and powder shown in the design.

45. The Grand Staircase

The staircase, characteristic of late sixteenth century work, was added at the same time as the interior of the Great Hall.

46. The Governors' Room

So called from the meetings of Governors of the Hospital formerly held in the room. Here, in all probability, Elizabeth and James kept their courts at the time of their respective visits to the Charterhouse. The mantelpiece and ceiling are both good and characteristic works. The decorations of the latter include shields with coats of arms of the Howards. The room contains some tapestry of the Duke of Norfolk's time. A portion is shown on the right of the photograph.

47. Entrance to the Chapel

The work is of Thomas Sutton's time. The room to which this is the entrance contains plaques commemorating the great who were scholars at the Charterhouse. As time passed and fees rose to twice the yearly income of a labourer in continuous employment, the pious wishes of Thomas Sutton regarding the education of the poor were put aside.

48. Founder's Tomb

This costly tomb, built mainly of alabaster, was not completed till 1615. The columns and arch shown in the photograph will convey a sufficient indication of the character of the architecture in the Chapel. The tomb is placed in a corner so dark that it needed a great deal of perseverance and all Mr. Dixon's skill to secure a satisfactory negative of this subject. 'The boys are already in their seats with smug fresh faces and shining white collars; the old black-gowned pensioners are already on their benches; the Chapel is lighted, and Founder's tomb, with its grotesque carvings and monster heraldries, darkles and shines with the most wonderful shadows and lights. There he lies, Fundator Noster, in his ruff and gown, awaiting the great examination day.' (Thackeray, in The Newcomes.*)*

37. General view from Charterhouse Square

38. Washhouse Court

39. Washhouse Court

40. The Cloisters

41. Second court with a view of the exterior wall of the Great Hall

41a. Inner Gate from first to second court

42. Interior

43. Interior, looking towards the screen and musicians' gallery

44. Chimney-piece

45. The Grand Staircase

46. The Governors' Room

47. **Entrance to the Chapel**

48. Founder's Tomb

SECTION 7
PHOTOGRAPHS OF SOUTHWARK AND ITS INNS, SION COLLEGE AND OXFORD MARKET

BY HENRY DIXON PRINTED IN
PERMANENT PIGMENTS FROM
HIS OWN NEGATIVES
FIRST ISSUED IN 1881

49. King's Head Inn yard
Demolished 1876

As there is but little to be said of the history of the 'King's Head', we may give here a specimen of Taylor, the Water Poet's, Carrier's Cosmographie, *written in 1637, and probably the earliest attempt at a Conveyance Directory: 'The carriers from Chittington, Westrum, Penborough, Slenge, Wrotham, and other parts of Kent, Sussex and Surrey do lodge at the "King's Head", in Southwark. They do come on Thursdays, and they go on Fridays'. The old Inn was burnt in the fire of 1676.*

50. The King's Head Inn yard
Demolished 1876

Until 1750 when Westminster Bridge was opened there was no way to cross the river but by London Bridge and no way to and from London Bridge but through Southwark. London was once a large manufacturing centre, while the counties south of the river were centres of heavy industry. Transport between London and the South passed through Southwark. By 1542 there were nineteen inns serving the carriers and travellers.

51. The White Hart yard
Demolished 1889

The most famous, next to the 'Tabard', of the inns of Southwark. Together they show the great extent at one time of this Inn and the depth of its fall from its 'most high and palmy state'. To the White Hart, Taylor, in his Carriers' Cosmographie *allots by far the longest list of carriers. Although, according to Mr. Rendle no part of the Inn as we see it is 200 years old, the White Hart dates back to the year 1400. Here half a century later in 1450, Jack Cade at the head of the commons of Kent, established his headquarters: 'the Kentish capteine being advertised of the king's advance, came first into Southwarke, and there lodged at the White Hart.'*

52. The inner yard of the White Hart
Demolished 1889

There are various literary references to the White Hart. Shakespeare in Henry VI, part 2, *has Cade say: 'Hath my sword, therefore broke through London Gates, that you should leave me at the White Hart, in Southwark?' One of the Paston Letters contains a vivid narrative of the rough doings at the White Hart, while occupied by Cade. To come much nearer to our times, the reader will not forget that Dickens, in the* Pickwick Papers, *gives a picture of the Inn as it was in the coaching days. It was here that bland Pickwick met his future servant, Sam Weller.*

53. The George Inn yard

The 'George' . . . is an old inn; it appears in Rendle's map. The comfortable inn has obviously been a good deal modernised since its rebuilding after the fire of 1676. Its large courtyard is now used as a railway goods office. The east and north galleries have been so boarded up as to lose all their old character.

54. The Queen's Head yard
Demolished 1886

We have seen that this Inn is mentioned by Stow. It does not appear in Rendle's map, where, however, we find occupying apparently the same site, the 'Crowned' or 'Crossed Keys', a sign derived from St. Peter's Keys. It seems probable that, the old sign perhaps growing out of favour with the progress of reformed religion, the Inn was rechristened after the Virgin Queen.

55. Entrance to the Queen's Head
Demolished 1886

A great fire in 1676 destroyed almost all of the inns in Southwark. So great was the destruction that boundaries had to be redrawn by a commission set up for the purpose.

56. Old houses in Borough High Street, Southwark
Demolished

An interesting group of eighteenth century houses.

57. St. Mary Overy's Dock
Demolished

'The dock', says Mr. Rendle 'exists in the very earliest maps . . . it was generally neglected and a nuisance, and must have been very much larger than we have known it to be.' None of the houses shown in the photograph are of any great age but altogether this is a quaint and interesting nook of Old London. The flat-headed doorway to the spectator's left, adjoining one with a round head, is, little as it looks like it, a busy public thoroughfare for pedestrians, unless a low swing-door is understood as reserving private rights. The passage, turning to the left through the houses leads to Clink Street. In a granary close by is a

large pointed arch, not visible from the outside, the last relic of what was once one of the most magnificent palaces in the land — Winchester House.

58. Old houses in Bermondsey Street
Demolished 1891

One cannot help speculating as to the origin of this singular group of houses, with their eight gables. Mr. Rendle, who was good enough to take great pains — unfortunately fruitless — to glean something for me about the history of these houses, tells me that in the early part of this century, houses of this type were exceedingly common in the main thoroughfare and bye places of Southwark. They are good specimens of the houses of the time of Elizabeth and somewhat later; the frame of massive timber, else mere shells of lathe and plaster; but though often out of shape and leaning in all directions, wonderfully durable.

59. Sion College, London Wall
Demolished 1886

Sion College stands on the site of Elsing Spital, a priory founded in 1332 by William Elsing, mercer of London. At the dissolution of religious houses it was granted to the Master of the King's Jewels. The house was burnt down in 1541 and no doubt rebuilt soon after. In 1623 it was purchased as a college for the clergy, and almshouses for twenty poor men and women under the provisions of the will of Dr. Thomas White, Vicar of St. Dunstan's in the West. The library was founded at the sole expense of Rev. John Simpson, one of Dr. White's executors. The greater part of the building was destroyed in the Great Fire of 1666, and the whole is usually said to have been rebuilt at different times later; but there are clear traces of Tudor work in the entrance, shown in the photograph.

On the opposite side of the street, seen through the gateway, is the old burying ground of St. Alphage, the site of the former parish church, bounded on the north side by a portion of the old city wall.

60. Oxford Market
Demolished 1880

Oxford Market was built about 1724, but not opened till 1732 (Allen's London). In Strype's Stow (1754) it is said to be 'not much resorted to at present,' a condition in which it seems to have remained till its demolition in 1880.

Nevertheless in the course of its existence it furnished a steak which alone should preserve its memory — that on which Burke was regaled by Barry, living then in 36 Castle Street, from the corner of which our photograph is taken. 'Sir,' said Barry, 'you know I live alone, but if you will come and help me eat a steak, I shall have it tender and hot from the most classic market in London — that of Oxford.' The day and the hour came, and Burke, arriving at No.36 Castle Street, found Barry ready to receive him. The fire was burning brightly, the steaks were put on to broil, and Barry, having spread a clean cloth on the table, put a pair of tongs into the hands of Burke saying, 'Be useful, my dear friend and look to the steaks till I fetch the porter.' Burke did as he was desired; the painter soon returned with the porter in his hand, exclaiming, 'What a misfortune! the wind carried away the fine foaming top as I crossed Titchfield Street. 'They sat down together; the steak was tender and done to a moment, the artist was full of anecdote, and Burke often declared that he had never spent a happier evening in his life. (Allan Cunningham, Lives of British Artists, quoted in Peter Cunningham's Handbook of London.) Dr. Johnson at one time lived at No. 6 in this same street, then on the verge of London towards the north.

49. King's Head Inn yard

Demolished 1876

50. The King's Head Inn yard

Demolished 1876

51. The White Hart yard

Demolished 1889

52. The inner yard of the White Hart
Demolished 1889

53. The George Inn yard

54. The Queen's Head yard

Demolished 1886

55. Entrance to the Queen's Head

Demolished 1886

56. Old houses in Borough High Street, Southwark

Demolished

57. St. Mary Overy's Dock

Demolished

58. Old houses in Bermondsey Street

Demolished 1891

59. Sion College, London Wall

Demolished 1886

60. Oxford Market

Demolished 1880

SECTION 8
PHOTOGRAPHS OF ASHBURNHAM HOUSE AND BANQUETING HOUSE, AND LINCOLN'S INN FIELDS

BY HENRY DIXON PRINTED IN PERMANENT PIGMENTS FROM HIS OWN NEGATIVES FIRST ISSUED IN 1882

61. Little Deans yard

The photograph shows the entrance to the quadrangle from the cloisters of Westminster Abbey. The arched doorway on the right surmounted by a pediment, is the entrance to Westminster School. A portion of the east wing of Ashburnham House is to be seen on the left. It would be difficult to find a more picturesque corner. By wonderful gradations resembling more the results of growth than of design, gables and roofs rise above one another till they culminate in the pinnacles of the South Transept of the Abbey, and the polygonal roof of the Chapter House.

62. Ashburnham House

The upper storey is a recent addition

The house is supposed to have been built for one of the Ashburnham family, probably for John Ashburnham, the attendant on Charles I from Oxford to the Scotch army, and from Hampton Court to the Isle of Wight. At all events it was in possession of the family at the beginning of the eighteenth century (Hatton's New View), and so remained till 1730, when it was purchased by the Crown, of John, the third Lord and the first Earl. The Cottonian Manuscripts were kept there, when in October, 1731, a fire broke out which nearly proved fatal to the entire collection. (Report from the Parliamentary Committee appointed to view the Cottonian Library, 1732.) In 1739 the house came into the possession of the Dean and Chapter of Westminster, who have lately been deprived of it by the operation of the Public Schools Act of 1868.

63. The Stairway

The stairway is mentioned in **Batty Langley's** *Ancient Masonry*, 1736.

This Staircase is now standing in a house adjoining to the Cloysters of Westminster Abbey wherein the Right Hon. the Earl of Ashburnham lately dwelt, and which Staircase his Lordship did inform me was built by Mr. Webb, a disciple of Inigo Jones, not by Inigo Jones himself, though perhaps the design might have been made by Inigo Jones and executed by Mr. Webb. In its upper Part is a sheroidical Dome, supported by small Columns on Pedestals, between which are Ballusters, and, if I mistake not, a gallery within them. The whole is not large, and of the Ionick Order, and which would have a better Effect than it now hath, was it of greater Dimensions; and, indeed if the upper Order of Columns that sustain

the Dome, had been made of the Corinthian Order, it would have been more masterly and better Architecture than it now is, where the Ionick on the Ionick seems to be absurd.

64. Archway, approach to the stairway

The Staircase, the most remarkable feature of the house, has always been deservedly admired for the ingenuity of its plan and the beauty of its design. It is surmounted, as Batty Langley states, by an oval dome and lantern. Sir John Soane had some very large drawings made of the Staircase, in illustration of his lectures at the Royal Academy. In more than one passage of these lectures he speaks in terms of high praise of the Staircase. The drawings and manuscript lectures are preserved in the Soane Museum. There are also in the Library of the Royal Institute of British Architects careful measured drawings of this Staircase, and engravings of it are given in Britton and Pugin's Public Buildings of London. *Those of Ware and Batty Langley have already been mentioned.*

65. The ante-room

The uppermost landing of the staircase gives direct access to the Dining Room and to the Ante-Room, which by a beautiful doorway communicates with the Drawing Room. The latter has a very rich ceiling of Jones's work, formerly, as shown by Sir John Soane's drawing (of about 1812), surmounted by a small oval or lantern, removed, no doubt, when the upper storey was added.

66. The dining room

The alcove is evidently by a later architect than Jones. This is also figured in Ware's book in an engraving, the only one in the book to which no architect's name is attached. The omission is certainly intentional, and Ware's practice in this matter leads me to the inference that he intended thus to indicate that the design was his own. It is thus that, in his Complete Body of Architecture, *his own designs for Chesterfield house and other buildings are given anonymously.*

67. The garden

The wall seen in the photograph, forming the northern boundary of the garden, is the wall of the Refectory of Westminster Abbey. The lower arcade with round-headed arches, remains of which are still visible in places, if of the time of

Edward the Confessor or of the first Norman Kings, the upper is of the time of Edward III. In this magnificent chamber, extending along the whole length of the South Cloister of the Abbey, the Commons not unfrequently assembled. 'In the first instance the two houses met in Westminster Hall, but they parted as early as the eleventh year of Edward I. From that time the Lords met in the painted chamber of the Palace, known also as King Edward's Chamber, the room where the Confessor died; and the Commons, whenever they sat in London, henceforward met within the precincts of the Abbey. On a few occasions they were assembled within the vast oblong Hall of the Refectory.' (Dean Stanley, Memorials of Westminster Abbey.)

The small summer house on the left of the picture is by Inigo Jones. Some think Jones's small buildings are his best, this one being so admired by Brettingham that he claimed it as his own in his *Plans of Holkham* 1773.

68. The Banqueting House, Whitehall

The Banqueting House was built from the designs of Inigo Jones in 1619-1622. 'The account', says Peter Cunningham, 'was not declared (i.e. finally settled) till the 29th June 1633, eleven years after the completion of the building, and eight after the death of King James, a delay confirmatory of the unwillingness of both father and son to bring the works at Whitehall to final settlement.' The Banqueting House is in truth but a fragment of a magnificent design. The following rhapsody is instructive, as showing the value set on Jones's work in the last century; it is from Campbell's Vitruvius Britannicus. 'This incomparable piece was designed by the immortal Jones, as one Pavillion for that admirable Model he gave for a Royal Palace and if this specimen has justly commanded the Admiration of Mankind, what must the finished Pile have produced? I hope Britain will still have the Glory to accomplish it, which will as far exceed all the Palaces of the Universe, as the Valour of our Troops and Conduct of our Generals have surpassed all others. Here our excellent Architect has introduc'd Strength with Politeness, Ornament with Simplicity, Beauty with Majesty; it is without Dispute the first Structure in the World, and was built Anno 1619.'

69. The water gate of York House
Preserved by the G.L.C.

The society used an earlier negative for this photograph as the building of Victoria Embankment made the gate difficult to photograph. The water gate was erected by the First Duke of Buckingham in 1626. Inigo Jones was originally thought to be its designer, but it is now attributed to Sir Balthasar Gerbier.

70. Archway to Clare Market
Demolished 1911

Renaissance ideas begin to influence architecture in this and other buildings in Lincoln's Inn Fields. The building is considered as a unified whole that does not permit additions and alterations. Up to this time architecture had an organic design, buildings being modified as the need arose.

In 1618, James I appointed a commission to plan the layout of Lincoln's Inn Fields:

'Know yee that it is noe small Contentment unto Us that, within theis sixteene Yeares of our Raigne over our Kingdome of England there have been more publique Works neer and about our Citie of London undertaken and finished then in Ages heretofore.' He goes on: 'And that the said Closes and Groundes commonlie called Lincolnes Inne Feildes, according to your Wisdoms and Discretions may be framed and reduced both for Sweetnes, Uniformite and Comlines into such Walkes, Partitions, or other Plottes, and in such sort, manner and forme, both for publique Health and Pleasure, as by the said Inago Jones is or shall be accordingly drawne by way of Mapp, or Ground Plott, exhibited plained and set out and approved by Us.'

71. Lindsey House

Virtue's notebooks give Inigo Jones as the designer but some people now attribute it to Nicholas Stone. *Lindsey House, sometimes called Ancaster House, after a subsequent owner, is assigned to the year 1640. It was built by Inigo Jones for Robert Bertie, Earl of Lindsey, who fell on the King's side at the battle of Edgehill. Hatton, writing in 1708, thus describes the house: 'Lindsey (the Lord) his Dwellinghouse is on the W. side of Lincolns-Inn Fields, a handsome building of the Ionick Order, and strong beautiful Court Gate, consisting of 6 fine spacious Brick Peers with curious Iron-work between them, and on the Peers are placed very large and beautiful Vases.' (New View.) An elevation in Campbell's Vitruvius Britannicus shows that the house has been much altered. The stone front is now plastered and painted, the entrance door has been widened, the windows cut down. and six urns removed from the balustrade.*

72. Newcastle House

Newcastle House, originally known as Powis House, is described by Hatton: 'Powis House, a noble spacious building, pleasantly situated at the N.W. angle of Lincolns-Inn Fields (or Great Square) strong and well built of Brick and Stone, adorned with a Pediment, Shield, Festoon etc. It was erected by the late Lord Powis about An. 1686, and being lately purchased by the Duke of Newcastle, is now in his Grace's own possession.' (New View.) *It was designed by Captain William Winde or Wynne, as he is called by Campbell in the* Vitruvius Britannicus *who there gives an engraving of his principal work, Buckingham*

House. Little or nothing is known of Winde but that he was a native of Holland and a pupil of Balthasar Gerbier. (Walpole, Ancedotes of Painting *ed. 1849.) It would be unfair to judge Winde's capabilities by Newcastle House as we now see it. An engraving in Strype's* Stow *(ed. 1754) shows it with a low stone wall where now are the iron railings; a stone balcony leads to the entrance door, which has a pediment; above the windows of the second floor is a rich cornice, in its centre a pediment - altogether a stately enough house.*

Lutyens' Newcastle House is in keeping with Winde's original without being a copy of it. A sensitive new building in keeping with the old one and its surroundings often looks good when a copy would look false. Thus there is a sense of artificiality about the new Lincoln's Inn gate despite the great care taken in its reproduction.

61. Little Deans yard

62. Ashburnham House

Upper storey is a recent addition

63. The Stairway

64. Archway, approach to the stairway

65. The ante-room

66. The dining room

67. The garden

68. The Banqueting House, Whitehall

69. The water gate of York House

Preserved by the G.L.C. in the Embankment Gardens

70. Archway to Clare Market

Demolished 1911

71. Lindsey House

72. Newcastle House

SECTION 9
PHOTOGRAPHS OF LAMBETH PALACE AND OLD HOUSES IN GREAT ORMOND STREET, CHEAPSIDE AND ALDGATE

BY HENRY DIXON PRINTED IN PERMANENT PIGMENTS FROM HIS OWN NEGATIVES FIRST ISSUED IN 1883

NOTES TO PLATES 73–84

73. Lambeth Palace Gate House
The tower was built by Morton between 1486-52. His rebus 'Mon a Ton' still remains on a leaden waterpipe. One of the best Tudor brick buildings in existence.

74. The Great Hall
Rebuilt in 1660-63 by Juxon who would not be swayed by Modernists and built the Hall to the original design.

75. The Lollards Tower or Water Tower
Completed in 1435 by Archbishop Chichley and constructed in ragstone at the cost of £291 19s. 4½d.

76. Old house opposite the Palace
Demolished 1889
The house, was said to have formed part of an old inn; the yard could be entered by the archway seen in the centre of the house.

77. Shambles in Aldgate
Demolished 1880
These houses were demolished to make way for the Metropolitan railway from Aldgate to Tower Hill.

78. An old inn in Aldgate
Demolished 1894
The courtyard of The Saracen's Head in Aldgate was used as a goods depot until its demolition.

79. The Golden Axe in St. Mary Axe
Demolished 1882
An overhanging gabled house on a timber frame.

80. No. 37, Cheapside
Demolished 1928
A house said to date from before the fire of 1666, built on the site of the Nag's Head Tavern. The tavern was famous during the controversies over the validity of Anglican Orders as the scene of the consecration of Archbishop Parker.

81. No. 73 Cheapside
Demolished 1928
The design is attributed to Sir Christophen Wren. It was built about 1668-69.

82. Old house, Great Ormond Street
Demolished 1882
An example of the Queen Anne Style. The portico was given to the South Kensington Museum, now the Victoria and Albert Museum.

83. Old house, Queen Square, Bloomsbury
Demolished
This house has been attributed, though not conclusively, to Sir Christopher Wren.

84. Shop, Macclesfield Street, Soho
Demolished 1885
This shop, built in 1690, was known to architects as the oldest shop in London.

73. Lambeth Palace Gate House

74. The Great Hall

Rebuilt in 1660-63 by Juxon

75. The Lollards Tower or Water Tower

76. Old house opposite the Palace

Demolished 1889

77. Shambles in Aldgate

Demolished 1880

78. An old inn in Aldgate

Demolished 1894

79. The Golden Axe in St. Mary Axe

Demolished 1882

80. No. 37, Cheapside

Demolished 1928

81. No. 73, Cheapside

Demolished 1928

82. Old house, Great Ormond Street

Demolished 1882

83. Old house, Queen Square, Bloomsbury

Demolished

84. Shop, Macclesfield Street, Soho

Demolished 1885

SECTION 10 PHOTOGRAPHS OF THE OLD BELL HOLBORN AND OLD HOUSES IN FLEET STREET, FORE STREET, GREAT WINCHESTER STREET, COLLEGE STREET AND AUSTIN-FRIARS

BY HENRY DIXON PRINTED IN
PERMANENT PIGMENTS FROM
HIS OWN NEGATIVES
FIRST ISSUED IN 1884

85. Old houses in Fleet Street
Demolished 1892

Aubrey tells us that Michael Drayton, the poet 'lived at the bay-windowe house, next the East end of St. Dunstan's Ch. in Fleet-Street' (Lives). Tradition claims for the house shown in the middle of the photograph the honour of having been the residence of the author of Polyolbion. *The Great Fire stopped, on the North side of Fleet Street, at Fetter Lane, sparing St. Dunstan's and the intervening block of houses. The house certainly dates from before the fire, and it agrees with Aubrey's description.*

86. Entrance to the Old Bell, Holborn
Demolished 1897

'The arms carved in stone, let into the front, are those of Sir Thomas Fowler, one of the Fowlers of Islington, a great family and Lords of the Manor of Barnsbury in the reigns of Elizabeth and James I.' (Lewis's History of Islington.*) The 'Old Bell' still retains something of its renown as a coaching Inn. The passer-by may note, in the summer months, placards announcing the hours of departure and arrival not only of the omnibus but of an occasional coach - not one of the amateur revivals of the last few years, but a genuine coach, a survival from the days before railways.*

87. The Old Bell, courtyard
Demolished 1897

The 'Old Bell' has been a favourite with more than one novelist. Mr. William Black has introduced it in his Strange Adventures of Phaeton, *where he speaks of 'The Old Bell Inn in Holborn, an ancient hostelry, which used in bygone times, to send its relays of stage coaches to Oxford, Cheltenham, Enfield, Abingdon, and a score of other places. Now from the quaint little yard, which is surrounded by frail and dilapidated galleries of wood, that tell of the grandeur of other days, there starts but a solitary omnibus, which daily whisks a few country people and their parcels down to Uxbridge, and Chalfont, and Amersham, and Wendover.'*

88. St. Giles, Cripplegate
The houses in the foreground were demolished in **1901. A statue of Milton now stands on the site.**
The photograph shows the tower of the Church, the body of which on the side of the street is masked by picturesque houses. The Church contains a modern bust of Milton who was buried here. In the churchyard, at one time, as may be seen by Archer's Vestiges, *very picturesque, but now spoilt by the erection around it of great warehouses, is a bastion, one of the few remaining fragments of London Wall.*

89. Old houses in Fore Street
Demolished 1883

The house, of a type very rare in London - made rarer still by the demolition of this subject – dates probably from before the Great Fire. In old times great fires often ravaged London but the lesson which they taught, only partly learnt, was too soon forgotten. Thus Stow tells us: 'Of old time, according to a decree made by Richard I, the houses of London were built of stone for defence of fire, which kind of building was used for two hundred years or more, but of later time, for winning of ground, taken down and houses of timber set up in place.' A Proclamation issued after the Great Fire, again forbade, under severe penalties, the building of timber houses. Experience had shown 'the notable benefit of brick which in so many places hath resisted and even extinguished the fire;' in this respect far better even than stone. It was therefore ordered 'that no man whatsoever shall presume to erect any house or building, great or small but of brick or stone; and if any man shall do the contrary, the next Magistrate shall forthwith cause it to be pulled down, and such further course shall be taken for his punishment as he deserves.'

90. Old house in Great Winchester Street
Demolished 1890

We have here, as in No. 20, the residence of a great merchant of the beginning of the 18th century. Great Winchester Street was full of such houses, as we read in the Stow of 1720: *'Here was a great Messuage called the Spanish Ambassador's House, of late inhabited by Sir James Houblon, Kt., and Alderman of London – he was also Governor of the Bank of England – 'and also other fair houses of Sir John Buckworth, and other Merchants.'*

91 Austin-Friars
Demolished 1896

The house, No.10, is a good example of a genuine Queen Anne; its date, 1704, is seen on the rain-pipe.

92. Austin-Friars
Demolished 1896
The staircase has a painted ceiling, the only one, perhaps yet left in a City house.

93. Doorways, Lawrence Pountney Hill
The finest early eighteenth century houses in the City are still in unspoilt condition although No.2 has an unfortunate addition.

94. College Street
Damaged by bombs in the Second World War
A view toward St. Michael Paternoster Royal.

Rebuilt by Wren in 1686-94, the steeple is a later addition (c. 1713). Bombs damaged the church and most of its fittings were destroyed.

95. Innholders' Hall
The street front, by J. Douglass Matthews, is plain apart from the ornate eighteenth century wooden door case.

96. Doorway in College Hill
This doorway, probably built as a merchant's residence still remains one of the best examples of late seventeenth century work in the City.

85. Old houses in Fleet Street

Demolished 1892

86. Entrance to the Old Bell, Holborn

Demolished 1897

87. The Old Bell courtyard

Demolished 1897

88. St. Giles, Cripplegate

The houses in the foreground were demolished in 1901

89. Old houses in Fore Street
Demolished 1883

90. Old house in Great Winchester Street
Demolished 1890

91. Austin-Friars

Demolished 1896

92. Austin-Friars
Demolished 1896

93. Doorways, Lawrence Pountney Hill

94. College Street

Survived bomb damage in the Second World War

95. Innholders' Hall

96. Doorway in College Hill

SECTION 11
PHOTOGRAPHS OF
THE INNS OF
COURT AND SIX
SMALL SUBJECTS

BY HENRY DIXON PRINTED IN
PERMANENT PIGMENTS FROM
HIS OWN NEGATIVES
FIRST ISSUED IN 1885

97. Inner Temple gateway
Now restored to its 1611 appearance
The plumes of feathers in the panels between the first and second floors were intended as a compliment to Henry, Prince of Wales. The statement conveyed by the inscription surrounding the picture of a 'hair-cutting saloon' that was 'formerly the palace of Henry VIII and Cardinal Wolsey' – not merely a palace but the *palace – must be taken as an example of unusually 'bold advertisement'. The assertion can only be accounted for by supposing that the author of the inscription confused this Gatehouse with that of the Middle Temple, with which, as will be seen, Wolsey's name is indeed connected.*

98. Churchyard Court
The court lies to the North of the Temple Church; the house against which the tombs are placed is that of the Master of the Temple. The tomb with the recumbent figure is that of John Hiccocks; that with the bust of Samuel Mead, both removed from the Church (Allen's History of London). *The tomb in the foreground is that of Oliver Goldsmith, placed here in 1860. The great writer was actually buried in this churchyard, but the exact position of his grave is uncertain.*

99. No. 5, King's Bench Walk
The houses are of red brick, all with fine doorways. The finest is perhaps that of no. 5, with its Corinthian pilasters.

100. Middle Temple gateway
Designed by Roger North in 1684, the gateway has four giant Ionic pilasters supporting a pediment on a brick main structure.

101. Fountain Court
Fountain Court 'is adorned', says Hatton, 'with an excellent fountain of water, which is kept in so good order as always to force its Stream to a vast and almost incredible altitude. It is fenced with Timber Pallisadoes, constituting a Quadrangle, wherein grow several lofty trees, and without are Walks extending on every side of the Quadrangle, all paved with Purbeck, very pleasant and delightful.' (New View Of London.)

102. Interior of Middle Temple Hall
Restored after bomb damage in the Second World War

Middle Temple Hall, one of the finest works of the Renaissance in England, was built between 1562 and 1572; the date 1570 appears in the window shown in the photograph. This date destroys the tradition that the screen was built from the spoils of the Spanish Armada, which put to sea only several years later. In addition to its beauty, the Hall has a great claim to our interest, in that the first record we have of Shakespeare's Twelfth Night *is contained in an entry in the diary of a student of the Middle Temple of a performance of the play in this Hall: 'Feb. 2, (1601-1602). At our feast we had a play called* Twelfth Night, or What you Will, *much like the* Comedy of Errors, or Menechmi *in* Plautus; *but more like and neer to that in Italian called* Inganni. *A good practice in it to make the steward believe his lady widdowe was in love with him, by counterfayting a letter as from his lady, in general terms, telling him that she liked best in him, and prescribing his gesture in smiling, his apparaille, etc; and then when he came to practice, making him believe they took him to be mad.'*

103. Gray's Inn
Survived bomb damage in the Second World War
Gray's Inn takes its name from Edmund, Lord Gray of Wilton, by whom, in 1505, the manor of Portpoole, otherwise called Gray's Inn, four messuages, four gardens, the site of a windmill, eight acres of land, ten shillings of free rent, and the advowson of the Chantry of Portpoole, were sold to Hugh Denny. From him the Manor passed to the Prior and Covent of East Sheen. They leased it to certain students of the law who became tenants of the Crown when the property was seized on the suppression of the religious houses.

104. Gray's Inn Hall
Severely damaged in the Second World War
Gray's Inn Hall was built in 1560. As will be seen it resembles in character and arrangement the Halls of the Charterhouse and of the Middle Temple; all three are indeed of nearly the same date. There is a tradition that the tables partly shown in the photograph were presented by Queen Elizabeth, whose 'glorious, pious, and immortal memory' is solemnly drunk here on grand days.

105. Clement's Inn garden
Demolished 1886

The photograph shows the well-known Garden House, with the trim lawn before it and the sun-dial, sold in 1884 by the Ancients for twenty guineas. The background on the right shows a portion of New Inn, where the great Thomas More studied. The Doric pilasters and cornices of the ground and first floors of Garden House seem to show that it is generally of an earlier date than would be inferred from the windows and balconies. The figure of the Moor supporting the sun-dial was presented to the Inn by Holles, Lord Clare, who brought it from Italy.

106. Clifford's Inn
Clifford's Inn is called after the family of that name, the widow of Robert de Clifford having let it to a society of law students about the year 1337. The arrangement of the small garden is, as the reader will observe, singularly like that of Gray's Inn.

107. Staple Inn Hall
Rebuilt after bomb damage in the Second World War

The doorway is Strawberry Hill Gothic dated 1753, and the main building is thought to date back to about 1630.

108. Six small subjects
The photograph shows a small neat statue of Guy, Earl of Warwick, renowned in the days of King Athelstan for killing the Danish giant Collbrand. The figure below it, of a boy on what may be a pannier, is in Panyer Alley, Newgate Street. The stone bears a quaint inscription. The figure of a pelican is from the front of a house in Aldermanbury, while the figure of Queen Elizabeth is a relic of Ludgate. The little figure of the naval officer taking an observation is that of the wooden midshipman of *Dombey & Son* The last of these subjects is a small draped figure, another relic of the City Gates of which, so far as I know, this and the statue of Queen Elizabeth are the only existing remains.

97. Inner Temple gateway

Now restored to its 1611 appearance

98. Churchyard Court

99. No. 5, King's Bench Walk

100. Middle Temple gateway

101. Fountain Court

102. Interior of Middle Temple Hall

Restored after bomb damage in the Second World War

103. Gray's Inn

Survived bomb damage in the Second World War

104. Gray's Inn Hall
Severely damaged in the Second World War

105. Clement's Inn garden

Demolished 1886

106. Clifford's Inn

107. Staple Inn Hall

Rebuilt after bomb damage in the Second World War

108. Six small subjects

SECTION 12
PHOTOGRAPHS OF GREAT
ST HELEN'S BISHOPSGATE STREET, THE TENNIS COURT IN THE HAYMARKET, EMMANUEL HOSPITAL, QUEEN ANNE'S GATE AND VARIOUS CHIMNEY-PIECES AND SMALL SUBJECTS

BY HENRY DIXON PRINTED IN
PERMANENT PIGMENTS FROM
HIS OWN NEGATIVES
FIRST ISSUED IN 1886

109. St. John's Gate, Clerkenwall
Restored 1845-46
The gatehouse which was built of Kent ragstone still exists.

110. Old houses in the Strand
Demolished 1909
These houses were on the South side of the Strand, almost opposite the church of St. Mary-le-Strand. Much of the detail was of eighteenth century origin but the main structure was early Stuart.

111. Great St. Helen's Bishopsgate Street
The timber frame house on the left was demolished in 1894. Great St. Helens still remains.

112. Tennis Court, Haymarket
Demolished 1868
The tennis court was once part of Piccadilly Hall, a gaming house of around 1635.

113. Emmanuel Hospital, Westminster
Demolished 1892-93
These buildings were part of Lady Dacre's foundation of 1601 and were known as Lady Dacre's Almshouses.

114. Queen Anne's Gate
The houses in the photograph still exist.
They are brown brick with bandings between the storeys, and have wooden doors. Queen Anne's statue was originally placed against the wall on the east side of the square but by 1708 had already been moved.

115. Chimney-piece, Sessions House, Clerkenwell

116. Chimney-piece, Court House, St. Andrew's Holborn
The church was gutted in the Second World War The organ front from the church of St. Andrews was taken down and distributed around the chimney, the effect being so incongruous that it has been removed from the negative.

117. Chimney-piece Tallow Chandlers Hall
Rebuilt after the fire of 1672
The table at the left of the picture was rescued from the fire. The chimney-piece follows the custom of the time in leaving an oblong space above the mantel for a landscape painting. Many originals were destroyed in this way.

118. Court Room, New River Company

119. Three doorways

120. Five subjects
Chained bear, Hourglass at St Albans, Wood Street; Boy at Pie corner; London stone and the Clock at St. Dunstans, in Fleet Street. When photographed the clock was at Regents Park. It was later moved to its present position outside St. Dunstan's.

109. St. John's Gate, Clerkenwall

Restored 1845-46

110. Old houses in the Strand

Demolished 1909

111. Great St. Helen's, Bishopsgate Street

112. Tennis Court, Haymarket

Demolished 1863

113. Emmanuel Hospital, Westminster

Demolished 1892-93

114. Queen Anne's Gate

The houses in the photograph still exist

115. Chimney-piece, Sessions House, Clerkenwell

116. Chimney-piece, Court House, St. Andrew's Holborn

The church was gutted in the Second World War

117. Chimney-piece, Tallow Chandlers Hall

Rebuilt after the fire of 1672

118. Court Room, New River Company

Overleaf:

119. Three doorways

120. Five subjects